Too Many Hiccups!

Written by Susan Cornell Poskanzer ■ Illustrated by Susan Magurn

MODERN CURRICULUM PRESS

PROJECT DIRECTORS: Susan Cornell Poskanzer
Leslie A. Baranowski

EXECUTIVE EDITOR: Wendy Whitnah
ART DIRECTOR: Lisa Olsson
DESIGNER: creatives nyc, Inc.

Published by Modern Curriculum Press

MODERN CURRICULUM PRESS, INC.
299 Jefferson Road, Parsippany, NJ 07054
(800) 321-3106 / www.mcschool.com

This edition is published simultaneously in Canada by Globe/Modern Curriculum Press, Toronto.

ISBN 0-8136-1317-5 (STY PK)   ISBN 0-8136-1318-3 (BB)   ISBN 0-8136-1319-1 (SB)

6 7 8 9 10   00 99

"I have hiccups," hiccuped Helen.

As soon as I have hiccuped,

there's another one."

"Hold your breath," called Cal.
"Count to ten," cried Hal.

"Hop up and down," said Mary Lou. "When you're not looking, I'll say

"I hate hiccups," hiccuped Helen.
"Hiccups are no fun.

As soon as I have hiccuped,

there's another one."

"Try a cartwheel!" cried Coach Yee.
"That will help. You will see."

"Have a cold drink," said Miss Allen.
"You may have to gulp a gallon."

"I **hate** hiccups," hiccuped Helen.
"Hiccups are no fun.

As soon as I have hiccuped,

"HICCUP

there's another one."

"I **hate** hiccups," hiccuped Helen. "Will I hiccup till I drop?"

But just as Helen said the words,
she felt her hiccups stop.